ADAGIO CANTABILE
from Sonata No.8, Op.13 'Pathétique'

Composed by Ludwig Van Beethoven

Suggested Percussion:
Chime or Glockenspiel (Ch/Gl)
Chinese bells (CB)
Triangle (Tr)
Drum played with fingers (Dr)

Adagio cantabile

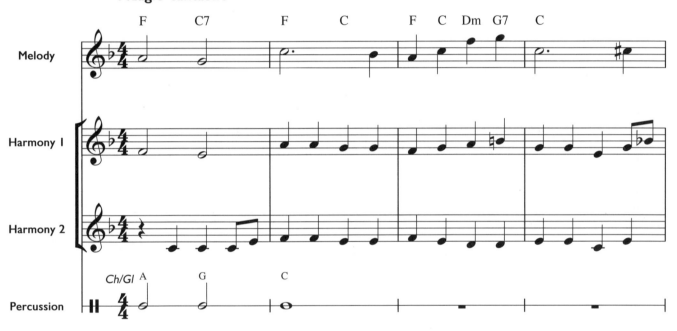

4

ANY DREAM WILL DO

from 'Joseph And The Amazing Technicolor® Dreamcoat'

Music by Andrew Lloyd Webber
Lyrics by Tim Rice

Suggested Percussion:
Shaker (Sh)
Tambourine (Tbn)
Woodblock (Wb)
Cymbal (Cym)

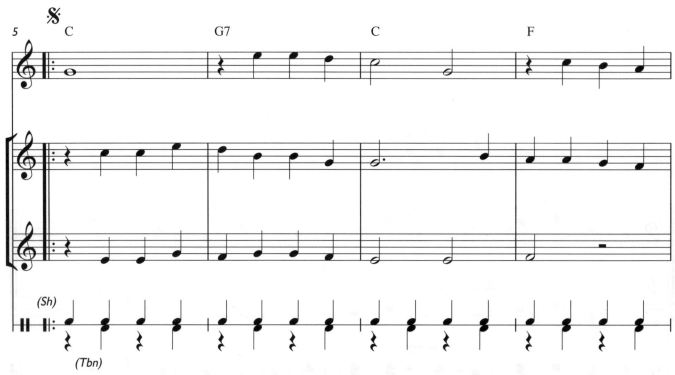

9

ANGELS

Words & Music by Robbie Williams & Guy Chambers

Suggested Percussion:
Glockenspiel (Gl)
Tambourine (Tbn)

Give Me Oil In My Lamp

Traditional

Suggested Percussion:
Chime or Glockenspiel (Ch/Gl)
Tambourine (Tbn)
Scraper (Scr)

Bright, with a swing

Joshua Fit De Battle Of Jericho

Traditional

Suggested Percussion:
Mixed group of untuned instruments.

STANDING IN THE NEED OF PRAYER

Traditional

Suggested Percussion:
Claves (Cl)
Tambourine (Tbn)

SWING LOW, SWEET CHARIOT

Traditional

Suggested Percussion:
Triangle (Tr)
Tambourine (Tbn)
Wood Block (Wb)
Cymbal (Cym)

24

D.S. al Coda

Coda

WITH A LITTLE HELP FROM MY FRIENDS

Words & Music by John Lennon & Paul McCartney

Suggested Percussion:
Shaker (Sh)
Tambourine (Tbn)
Cymbal played with a beater (Cym)

27

You Raise Me Up

Words & Music by Rolf Lovland & Brendan Graham

Suggested Percussion:
Chinese bells (CB)
Triangle (Tr)
Cymbal with beater (Cym)

Slow ballad tempo

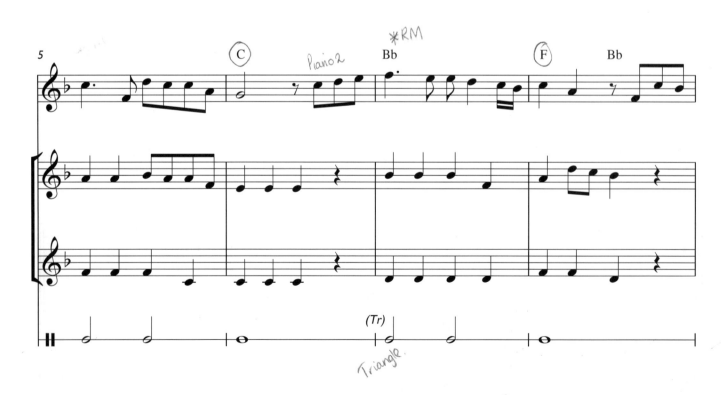

28

TOP OF THE WORLD

Words by John Bettis
Music by Richard Carpenter

Suggested Percussion:
Shaker (Sh)
Woodblock (Wb)
Tambourine (Tbn)

Moderately, with a bounce

31